God's
little book of
Hope

Words of inspiration and
encouragement for difficult times

Richard Daly

Collins

Collins, a division of
HarperCollins Publishers
77–85 Fulham Palace Road

First published in Great Britain in 2007
© 2007 Richard Daly

Richard Daly asserts the moral right to be identified as the author
of this work

A catalogue record for this book is available from the British
Library

ISBN-13: 978-0-00-724625-0

10 9 8 7 6 5 4

Printed and bound in Great Britain by
by Martins the Printers Ltd, Berwick upon Tweed
Typeset by MATS Typesetters, Southend-on-Sea, Essex

INTRODUCTION

In a time when things seem rather despairing and
when the news of the day often seems to be
nothing other than bad news, what hope is there?
Today there are people dying with no hope and,
perhaps even worse, people living without hope.

Yet such a seemingly dark and gloomy outlook
is not the be all and end all: there is a ray of hope.
We can experience life optimistically,
expecting a bright future. It is God's desire
that we live life abundantly.

I hope this volume will provide some possible
answers for life's worries, and enable you to
experience a life worth living!

HOPE IN GOD'S PROMISES

We could never keep every promise we've ever
made. But God is 100% faithful, Every one
of God's promises is 'yes' in Christ.

2 Corinthians 1:20

HOPE ON

Hope means hoping even when things
seem hopeless.

Joel 3:16

VALUE WHAT YOU HAVE

Never take a simple breath for granted.
It's a privilege to be alive.

In spite of all cruelty and unfairness, life
is beautiful, precious and an incredible gift.
Let us make the best of it.

Psalm 8:3–6

NEW DAWN, NEW HOPE

Hope forever tells us that
tomorrow will be better.

Lamentations 3:22–23

WHEN ALL ELSE FAILS, TRY JESUS

If you have been reduced to God as your
only hope, you're in a good place.

Psalm 3:3
Psalm 39:7

BE HOPEFUL IN HOPELESSNESS

As long as matters seem hopeful, hope remains merely superficial. It's only when everything is hopeless, that hope truly proves its strength.

Romans 8:24
Job 5:9

FIND HOPE WITHIN

'Life treasures are not far afield upon
some distant shore.
Jewels of peace and happiness are
found right at your door.'

Author unknown

Genesis 28:15

PERSEVERE

There are many lessons that can be learnt from
watching children learn to walk. Countless times
they fall, cry and are hurt, but still get back up
and try again. It's a sure reminder that what
we want to accomplish may not always
be easy. But persevere!

Matthew 24:13
Matthew 19:14

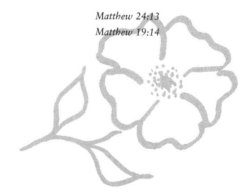

LET GOD LEAD

When the way forward seems a bit blurred, it can be God's way of getting you to recognise that things are changing. That's the time to consult him as to your next move.

Proverbs 3:5,6
Psalm 25:5

EXPLORE THE QUALITIES OF HOPE

Three relatives of hope:
Willingness – to accept whatever comes knowing
you'll come through stronger.
Determination – the ability to stand firm
while those around you are falling.
Insight – to see the character-developing
hand of God in it all.
With these qualities, you will survive!

Romans 5:3–4

DON'T SETTLE FOR SECOND BEST

Your biggest enemy is not the challenges you face;
it's compliancy, negativity, self-imposed
limitations and self-pity.
The Apostle Paul wrote 'I can do all things
through Christ who strengthens me'.
That means you can rise above circumstances,
if you want to.

Philippians 4:13
Proverbs 13:12

BE AN ENCOURAGER

The world is full of discouragers... what we need
is more encouragers. Many times a word of praise,
thanks or appreciation has kept a person
on their feet. Encourage someone today:
it will bring healing.

Proverbs 15:23
Isaiah 52:7

PRAYER CHANGES THINGS

When a believing person prays, great things
happen. When God prompts you to pray for
somebody, don't wait to do it! Your prayer may
be the only thing standing between
that person and catastrophe.

James 5:16

BE NOT DISMAYED

Remember, life will go on, even if it doesn't go according to your plan. Don't wait until you lose a loved one or have a heart attack before you discover that. Your worth comes from God, his opinion of you never changes.

Philippians 4:6

GIVE THANKS EVERY DAY

Finding time to pray every day will always
be a challenge, because prayer is a learnt
behaviour. So, when you wake up, say,
'Lord, thank you for giving me this new day.
Help me to rejoice and be glad in it.'

Psalm 100
Psalm 118:24

TAKE GOD AT HIS WORD

In life people will seek to offend you, for whatever reason. What's important is not what others say about you, it's what you say to yourself. Affirm yourself by the truth of God's word.

Psalm 139:16–18

LIVE TO YOUR POTENTIAL

You can never really tell what potential lies within,
until you have a purpose and a will to achieve
a goal. Life is an adventure; we get out
of it what we put into it.

John 10:10

LAUGHTER IS THE BEST MEDICINE

It's a fact: laughter increases immunity, and
benefits cardiovascular, respiratory, digestive
and muscular systems. It reduces pain and stress,
increases energy and gives you a sense of well
being. It's also contagious!

Proverbs 17:22
Ecclesiastes 3:4

BE PATIENT IN TRIBULATION

Happiness would not be fully appreciated without
an experience of its opposite, sadness. Consider
those who have experienced such adversity
and learn from them.

Romans 12:12

THINK HAPPY THOUGHTS

Happiness is a product of attitude and thought.
It comes from you, not to you. To be happy,
you must think happy.

Psalm 128:2

LOOK FOR OPEN DOORS

When one door closes,
God always opens another.

Revelation 3:8

DISPEL YOUR FEARS

The one great enemy of the human race is fear.
The less fear you have, the more health and
harmony you will have. Remember fear is a
bluffer, it boasts more than what it can really do.
Call its bluff, and it will disappear.

Isaiah 41:10–14

HOLD ON

One of the most common mistakes is thinking that success in life comes from some magical formula which we do not possess. Success is simply holding on and not letting go.

Revelation 3:11

DO SOMETHING CREATIVE

Develop a hobby. Do something for the sheer joy
of it. Those who develop a creative and absorbing
interest are better able to stand up to the stresses
and strains of life.

Colossians 3:23

WORK THROUGH YOUR PROBLEMS

Don't run away from a problem, face it.
Chisel it into small parts, and deal with
each part separately.

Matthew 11:28,29
Psalm 55:22

REMINISCE TO REJUVENATE

What are your happiest moments? Savour again an
event of past years, or a long ago thrill and some
of the original warmth of the occasion will return
to cheer the present.

Deuteronomy 32:7
Proverbs 10:7

THERE'S POWER IN PRAYER

Why pray? Because nothing lies beyond the reach
of prayer. You'll never know how many people
have been strengthened because you asked
God to encourage them.

James 5:16

DEVELOP AN ATTITUDE
OF GRATITUDE

Though your present situation may seem dismal,
develop an attitude of gratitude. It's surprising how
just giving thanks in all circumstances puts your
life into perspective.

1 Thessalonians 5:18

THE BLESSED HOPE

The greatest hope you can ever have as a follower
of Christ is the blessed hope of the glorious
return of Jesus Christ our Lord.

Titus 3:6–7
John 14:1–3

SOUL FOOD

There is a common saying, 'you are what you eat'.
In other words, to achieve good health we need
a balanced diet. Likewise, reading the Bible
gives spiritual food for our souls.

Deuteronomy 8:3

TRUST GOD'S TIMING

When God plants a dream in your heart, he starts
preparing you for its fulfilment. He strengthens
your character and deepens your spiritual roots.
Don't try to bring it to birth prematurely,
instead trust God's timing.

John 12:24

JUST FOR TODAY

This day will only come once. Challenge yourself
by saying, 'Just for today I will enjoy each moment
to the fullest, and try not to tackle all life's
problems at once. Just for today I will try to enjoy
every one of God's blessings.'

Psalm 118:24

CONSIDER YOUR VALUE

Do you realise that when you put yourself down,
you're insulting your maker? God says you are
fearfully and wonderfully made: in his eyes
you are just right.

Psalm 139:14
Ephesians 1:11

TRUST GOD

There is only one person who is ultimately faithful,
reliable and dependable and in whom we can fully
trust. As the Scriptures declare, 'Put not your hope
in man in whom there is no hope,
but put your hope in God.'

Psalm 146:3
Lamentations 3:24

HOLD ON

When it seems that your prayers are not being
answered, it may be that God is simply saying
'hold on'. During this time he will be healing your
past so it cannot pollute your future.

Isaiah 49:8

NOTHING IS TOO HARD FOR GOD

Nothing shocks God, or catches him off guard.
When the crisis you're facing makes you want to
throw in the towel, remember your problems
are his opportunities.

Matthew 19:26
Mark 14:36

LET IT GO

The word 'forgive' literally means 'to give away':
it has very little to do with the other person;
it's a decision you make, like exhaling carbon
dioxide from your body because you know
holding on to it will only harm you.
So go ahead, exhale: release forgiveness.

Matthew 6:12–15

START TODAY

The first step to pursuing joy is simply to begin.
The Psalmist says, 'This is the day that the
Lord has made; let us rejoice and be glad in it.'
If we wait until conditions are perfect,
it will never happen.

Psalm 118:24

Psalm 68:3

HOW PRECIOUS YOU ARE

The fact that God cares for you may be hard to hold on to when you are having a bad day; but to be cared for means to be wanted, and despite your failures, God still wants you. It's a truth that will never go away, so accept it!

John 15:15

LEARN TO RELAX

Hope fades when we constantly get uptight about everything: being five minutes late, getting stuck in traffic, waiting in line, overcooking a meal, gaining weight, discovering another grey hair. Lighten up – release the tension and let hope soar.

Romans 5:5
Ecclesiastes 3:12,13

GET STAYING POWER

In times of powerlessness it's comforting to know
that God gives power to the weak, and to those
who have no might, he increases strength.

Isaiah 40:29
Isaiah 61:1

MORE HOPE, LESS WORRY

The Bible says, 'The Lord is faithful, he will guard
you from evil.' You may not know what you're
being protected from, but God knows: he saves
your life every day! So trust him more, complain
less; hope in him more, and worry less.

2 Thessalonians 3:3
Psalm 103:4

CAPTURE NEGATIVE THOUGHTS

Low self-esteem arises when we listen to lies about ourselves. When a negative thought enters your mind, that could be crippling to your character, capture it, assess it, measure it up to what God thinks of you, and if it doesn't match up, throw it out!

2 Corinthians 10:5
Philippians 4:7

PUT YOUR FAITH TO THE TEST

When you are overwhelmed, it is easy to jump to the conclusion that God isn't on the job. When you can't figure it out, you have to faith it out!

Psalm 9:10–11

USE WHAT YOU'VE GOT

It's easy to use our limitations as an excuse for
doing nothing productive with our lives. But God
wants you to develop your strengths and fulfil your
life's purpose. So instead of dwelling on what you
don't have, start using what you have.

Ephesians 2:10

TAKE GOD AT HIS WORD

God has given us his 'promise and his oath' so in
prayer, even though you may not get the answer
you want, you can rest assured he makes
'everything work together for good'.

Hebrews 6:18
Romans 8:28

APPRECIATE YOURSELF

Everything God made was very good; that means
you, too. Endeavour to see yourself as God sees
you: he wants to change your self-image so you
can appreciate your unique gifts and qualities.

Genesis 1:31

CHERISH WHAT'S YOURS

Learning to be content with what we have puts
what we hope for in perspective. The last
commandment says 'do not covet'. Once we're
satisfied with what we've got, our hopes
will not be covetous.

Philippians 4:11
1 Timothy 6:8

ENJOY THE MOMENT

When you appreciate the moment, you instinctively
know that as long as you have life, you have hope.
Enjoy the moment.

Deuteronomy 4:4
Luke 19:9

CHOOSE TO BE HAPPY

Happiness is not something you pursue; indeed the
more you pursue it, the more elusive it becomes.
Happiness is something you can choose
to accept right now.

Psalm 128:2
Acts 26:2

BE OPTIMISTIC ABOUT LIFE

One of the discoveries of modern medicine is that the more optimistic you are, the greater your chances of maintaining health. Simply believe that you will be well: you've got nothing to lose.

Isaiah 65:18
Luke 6:23
James 5:13

PUT HOPE INTO ACTION

Some conclude that hope is merely an expectation of certain outcomes. It's more than this: hope is a real commitment to positive behaviour and attitudes. It's an active, positive word. Adapt this approach and live an abundant life.

Romans 15:13
Romans 12:12

BE CALM

A calm state of mind is naturally accompanied
by hope and optimism. Maintain the calm,
and you maintain the hope.

John 14:27
Romans 15:13

GET EXCITED ABOUT SOMETHING

Enthusiasm. What a wonderful action word! It is
an effective, contagious force. It helps you achieve
the impossible and makes the future full of
promise. Be enthusiastic!

Psalm 32:11
Psalm 47:1

GIVE, AND IT WILL COME BACK TO YOU

When you go out of your way to do good for others you derive a double benefit. First, any selfless act generates a feeling of well-being, and second, your outlook on life becomes more meaningful.

Luke 6:38
2 Corinthians 9:6–8

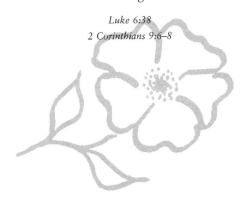

CELEBRATE LIFE

Your birthday is a wonderful opportunity to celebrate the miraculous achievement of what your life has been to date. If there's one thing that's worth celebrating, it's the fact that you are alive.

Luke 12:23
John 10:10

MAKE UP YOUR MIND

Abraham Lincoln said, 'A man is as happy
as he makes up his mind to be.' The same can
be said of hope: you're as hopeful as you make
up your mind to be.

Psalm 45:2
Psalm 71:5,14

GO BACK TO THE FUTURE

Generally, the problems of today become less
threatening with the course of time. If you imagine
yourself at some time in the future looking back on
your worries today, you'll discover they were not
worth worrying about at all.

Matthew 6:25–34

BE THE CHANGE

Gandhi once said, 'Be the change you want to see in the world.' There's no better place to begin than with yourself.

Psalm 51:10

TREASURE YOUR TREASURED MOMENTS

When you have an inspiring thought or experience, keep a journal to treasure these moments. Over a period of time you will build a collection of your own personal inspirations to refer to in times of need.

Isaiah 30:8
Jeremiah 30:2
Revelation 1:19

KEEP ON KEEPING ON

There is one trait that produces more positive
results than knowledge, wealth or fame –
persistence. If you just keep going, maintaining
your hope and belief that something good will
happen, eventually it will.

2 Timothy 4:5

CHANGE YOUR WAYS

It's never to late to change bad habits, unhelpful patterns of behaviour, fixed routines, or mundane cycles. All it takes is commitment, and a change of perspective, and you can alter the negative.

Philippians 3:21

LOOK FORWARD WITH HOPE

No matter how dark and dreary the days ahead
may seem, there is always something positive to
look forward to that can become your beam of
light. Just flick on the switch.

Hebrews 12:2

DON'T STAY DOWN

Life is all about learning from our mistakes; and
the beauty of it is that no matter how many times
we fail, there's always another chance. Failure is
not the falling down; it's the staying down.

Psalm 37:24

DON'T BE MISERABLE

Miserable people get the same number of
opportunities as happy people. They just tend to
overlook them. Look for the good and you'll feel
much more hopeful.

Isaiah 45:22

KEEP FIT, FEEL GOOD

As we know, exercise brings our body to an
overall state of good health. It also has benefits
spiritually. By giving us a vitality for life, exercise
gives us a more hopeful outlook. Isn't that
worth working up a sweat for?

3 John 2

TURN TO TH

Let the rays of the sun perm
Sunlight, apart from being
vitamin D, staves off those me
and injects hopefulness and vib

Matthew 13:4

YOU ARE WHAT YOU THINK

The words you use, like your thoughts, have
a powerful influence on how you behave.
Reinforce your positive behaviour by telling
yourself, 'there is much to live for',
'life does get better', 'there is hope'.

Proverbs 23:7

YOU ARE INDISPENSABLE

Remember, you are unique. There is no one else on
this planet like you. You are one of a kind, just as
important as anyone else in this world, and the
contribution you make is vital. So take your
rightful place on the podium.

Isaiah 43:2

SOW A LITTLE HOPE

The growth cycle of a plant reassures us of the continuity of life. Germination, the sprouting plant, its growth and its eventual natural recycling, all show us that there is order and purpose in life.

Psalm 126:6

ENDURE YOUR TEST

What may seem to you to be bitter trials are often
blessings in disguise. Take comfort in the hope that
when you come through, you will be stronger,
as gold tried in the fire.

1 Peter 1:7

RELAX YOUR FACE AND SMILE

Smiling relaxes your face. You use less facial
muscles than when frowning and communicate
good feelings toward others and within yourself.

Proverbs 15:13
Nehemiah 2:2

KEEP FOCUSED

When you have a purpose in life, you will be less
affected by the obstacles that come in your way.
Instead of seeing them as hindrances, they become
stepping stones to success.

Philippians 3:13,14

RELEASE YOUR POTENTIAL

Every new opportunity in life remains only
potential until you take that first step forward. Go
forward, take the first step, and the rest of the
journey will take care of itself.

Psalm 16:11
Psalm 119:105

THE SERENITY OF PRAYER

'God grant me the courage to change the things
I can, the patience to accept the things I can't,
and the wisdom to know the difference.'

James 1:5

IT GETS EASIER

It's always the beginning of a task that seems the
most challenging – riding a bike, playing the piano,
learning a language. It's most difficult just before
it starts to get easier. So take courage:
when it seems daunting, your life could
be about to turn for the better.

2 Timothy 2:3
Matthew 24:13

WAR OF THE MIND

You can think yourself into happiness or success,
despair or hopefulness. It all depends how you
manage the volume of one type of thought over
the other. The one that dominates the mind
tends to be the winner. The good thing is that
you decide who will win.

Isaiah 26:3
Luke 12:29

LOOK UP

It's only when we walk with our head down that
we bump into lamp posts – with our chin up and
head straight, in the dark the same lamp post
becomes our light and guide.

Micah 7:7

IT'S WORTH THE WAIT

On earth we have the pain without the reason.
In heaven we have the reason without the pain.

Revelation 21:4

GO FORWARD

There are many things in life that we have no
control over, especially things in the past.
Acknowledging these areas in life will enable
us to move forward and create new pathways
for the future.

Isaiah 38:17
Philippians 3:13

DON'T WORRY

The things we worry about rarely become a reality.
It's like dynamite without a flame to light it,
potentially destructive but actually powerless. In
fact, the only damage it does is rob you
of a hopeful tomorrow.

Philippians 4:6

THINK AHEAD

You limit your future when you dwell in the past.
You can accomplish a lot more by envisioning
your future plans. Actualise it in your mind,
see it before it happens.

Proverbs 23:4

TREAT OTHERS WELL

'Do unto others as you would have them do unto you'. The golden rule, if practised, can lead to a golden experience.

Micah 12:33
Leviticus 19:18

TAKE NOTHING FOR GRANTED

When you lower your assumptions of what you expect from other people, you will receive a welcome surprise. Assume nothing, but know that great things lie ahead for you.

Philippians 2:3

LESSONS FROM A BABY

The birth of a baby is the personification of hope.
It ought to remind you not only of a perfect
creator, but also a perfect sustainer of life.

Ecclesiastes 9:4
Romans 8:24

CHOOSE A POSITIVE RING TONE

Choose a ring tone that instils positive thoughts
every time it rings. Not only will you not mind
the phone ringing, but the words will reinforce
feelings of well being. How about
'I Feel Good' by James Brown!

2 Chronicles 7:6
1 Samuel 16:23

LOOK FOR THE GOOD

Despite our faults or failings, we all have
something positive that's worthwhile.
To discover it in those around you, just look
for it – but be aware, it may mean choosing
to ignore the negative.

Proverbs 12:25,15:23
1 Thessalonians 5:21

SHOW GENUINE LOVE

Amid so many rules and laws, we're told to abide by two commands: 'Love your God with all your heart', and 'Love your fellow men'. If we truly practise this, everything else will fall into place.

Mark 12:28–33

ACT WHAT YOU BELIEVE

When you act as though life has something special in store for you, you'll soon discover it's true. Not only is it a biblical promise, but you also convince your subconscious, and this becomes self-fulfilling.

Mark 9:23

'BIG UP' YOURSELF

If no one else is around to compliment you,
go ahead and do it yourself. Congratulate and
reassure yourself. If there's one person it pays
to have on your side, it's you!

Psalm 139:14

MAINTAIN YOUR FRIENDSHIPS

An important factor in inspiring you to be hopeful is the support of old friends. Treasure those associations – it's so easy to be 'out of sight, out of mind'. If you have an old friend, don't let them go.

Proverbs 17:17

DON'T NEGLECT GOD'S LEADING

Sometimes we forget the struggles we've been
through and how God helped us get through them.
Take time out today and reflect on how God has
helped you in the past. It will give you added
confidence for the future.

Isaiah 46:9

ALL THINGS BRIGHT AND BEAUTIFUL

If you want to inject feelings of brightness and jubilance, surround yourself with colourful flowers. The fragrance alone acts as a healing balm.

Isaiah 40:6

MAINTAIN YOUR INTEGRITY

The satisfaction of a job well done will bring
rewards of its own. If you work diligently and
faithfully, you not only feel a greater sense of
achievement, but contentment that you've done
your best, even if no one else notices.

Proverbs 13:11

READ MORE, WATCH LESS

Usually your imagination is more active when
you're reading than when you're watching. That's
why literature can have a more uplifting and long-
lasting effect than more passive mediums of
entertainment. Spend time reading books,
and let your imagination work.

2 Timothy 2:15

A PRAYER OF HOPE

Thank you Lord for filling my past and my present
with your love, your mercy and your grace. Thank
you for the promise that I can spend all my
tomorrows with you.

Hebrews 6:19

A POEM OF HOPE

'Be content, my heart, though you cannot see
God's vast eternal mystery.
Be at peace, my soul, like a child at rest,
in the simple truth that God knows best.'

2 Corinthians 4:16–18

A TIME TO DANCE

The wise king Solomon said, 'for everything there
is a season', and goes on to list many events in life.
When you've cried all your tears, dance. You'll be
surprised how therapeutic it can be.

2 Samuel 6:14
Psalm 30:11

HOPE IN GOD

Remember, God is not bound by our circumstances, neither is he overcome by our turmoil. In every situation he has power to provide a way out for you. Put your hope in him.

Psalm 121:1–3

THE HOPE OF THE WORLD

'Life with Christ is an endless hope,
without him a hopeless end.'

Anonymous

Philippians 1:20,21

LOOK UP

When looking backward is filled with pain
and looking forward seems ominous;
try looking upward.

Psalm 107:28–30

HOLD ON TO HOPE

'Today well-lived makes every tomorrow
a vision of hope.'

Anonymous

Romans 15:13

HOPE IN THE FUTURE

As a believer in God you can confidently say,
'Although I don't know what the future holds,
I know who holds the future!'

Deuteronomy 1:29–30

BE PROACTIVE

Don't wait for the opportunities to do good,
make the opportunities.

Colossians 1:10
Proverbs 12:25

YOU'RE NEVER ALONE

When you're alone, you can be certain of one
thing: even though you may not feel his presence,
God is with you – he will never
fail in his promises.

Joshua 1:5,6

A BEACON OF HOPE

'The world cries out with a common voice,
"Is there hope? Where can hope be?" To our
wounded world God still replies, "With the
cross of Calvary".'

B.J. Huff

Isaiah 55:3

DECIDE ON YOUR OWN ENDING

Do not think of your problems as a full stop,
but merely as a comma. You can decide how the
rest of the sentence will run.

Philippians 1:6

LET HOPE HEAL

In times of illness, the human body experiences a natural gravitational pull in the direction of hope. That's why the patient's hope is the physician's secret weapon. It is the hidden ingredient in any prescription.

Jeremiah 17:14

CAST YOUR CARES ON HIM

At the cross, Jesus took on all our sins and
troubles and placed them on himself. Yet the
sacrifice wasn't just a one-off, he is more than
willing to do it for you again and again.
What sacrificial love!

Romans 5:8

FEAR NOT

The fear of what might happen tomorrow is far
worse than the actual experience of any present
sorrow. Don't take upon yourself unnecessary pain.
Ask God to banish the fears.

Lamentations 3:57,58

FOCUS ON THE LITTLE THINGS

It is the little things that usually have the greatest impact in life – a compliment, a smile, a thank you, a hug. It's these things that make up a positive outlook.

Luke 19:17

NEVER GIVE IN

'Never give in, never give in. Never, never, never,
never – in nothing, great or small, large or petty,
never give in, except to convictions of honour
and good sense.'

Winston Churchill

Jeremiah 7:24
1 Thessalonians 5:21

START AFRESH

'Today is the first day of the rest of your life.'

Dale Carnegie

Proverbs 4:18
Psalm 118:24

HOPE IS LIFE

'What oxygen is to the lungs, such is hope
to the meaning of life.'

Emil Brumes

1 Timothy 4:9–10

ACT ON INSPIRATION

It's not inspiring books or presentations that change people's lives; they simply act as a catalyst. It is what you choose to believe and act upon, that's where the change comes. No one can change the life of any individual except that individual.

Joshua 24:15

CLAIM THE GIFT

'Yesterday's history,
Tomorrow's a mystery.
All we have is Today, and it's called the present
Because it's a precious gift.'

Anonymous

James 1:17

METAMORPHOSIS

What the caterpillar sees as the end, the butterfly
sees as just the beginning. It's the same life
with a new outfit.

2 Corinthians 5:17

YOU ARE WHO YOU ARE

When you start comparing yourself with others,
eventually you will become either resentful or vain,
for there will always be greater or lesser people
than you. Be yourself. Accept yourself.
Appreciate yourself!

1 Peter 2:9

ATTITUDE PROBLEMS

Your attitude dictates your whole approach to life.
The good news is, you can alter your life simply
by changing your attitude.

Psalm 37:5

TRUST YOURSELF

Intuition is the ability to discern based on instinct.
To many questions of your life, the answers really
lie within. Instead of constantly listening to others
– listen to yourself. You are your own solution.

Isaiah 30:21

GET UP AGAIN

Falling down is a temporary condition. Staying down is what makes it permanent.

Isaiah 37:24
Micah 7:8

DON'T LET GO

'When you get to the end of the rope,
tie a knot and hold on.'

Franklin D. Roosevelt

1 Thessalonians 5:21

FLEE TEMPTATION

We are promised that in every tempting situation, there is always a way of escape. Don't get caught, look for the exit.

1 Corinthians 10:13
Revelations 3:10

HERE TODAY, GONE TOMORROW

'And it came to pass', is a common phrase in the
Old Testament. It is a reminder that, whatever our
present turmoil – be hopeful, it too will pass.

2 Samuel 11:1,2
Romans 8:18

BELIEVE, AND YOU WILL

If you believe you can, you can
If you believe you can't, you can't
So what do you want to believe?

Mark 11:24
Mark 9:23

LEAVE IT TO GOD

'If we have faith the size of a mustard seed, we can move mountains.' Don't look at the mountain, look to the Mountain Mover.

Matthew 17:20
Matthew 21:21

DAILY GUIDANCE

'Lord, let me live one day at a time.
My choice determined by your will,
My path illumined by light,
My faith grounded in your truth,
My heart set on eternity.'

Proverbs 4:11

EXPECT THE UNEXPECTED

If you travel a path in life without obstacles, you're probably going around in circles. The only guaranteed thing in life is its unexpectednesses.

John 16:33

DO IT EVEN WHEN AFRAID

Facing our fears is sometimes the hardest thing to do. Not everything that is faced can be changed, but nothing can be changed unless it is faced.

Isaiah 41:10
Exodus 14:13

TRY NOTHING, GAIN NOTHING

What would you attempt to do if you knew
you would fail? What would you lose
if you never attempted? In every attempt
there's always a lesson.

1 Samuel 17:32
Luke 22:33

COUNT YOUR BLESSINGS

The words of the hymn writer still ring true,
'Count your blessings, name them one by one...
and it will surprise you what the Lord has done'.
That's one hymn worth putting into practice!

Ephesians 1:3
Malachi 3:10

LEARN YOUR LESSONS

When you've come through your test in life,
commune with God to discover what lesson
he would have you learn.

Psalm 25:4

TURN A MINUS TO PLUS

Find courage in dis-courage-ment.
An appointment in dis-appointments and
hope in hope-lessness.

Job 41:22
Psalm 30:11

BE PATIENT

Whether it's the best of times or the worst of
times, remember there are other times to come.

Psalm 30:5

LOOK TO THE CROSS

We all have our crosses to bear, some large, some
small, but because of the cross Christ carried,
we all have the hope of eternal life.

1 John 2:25

TURN IT OVER TO JESUS

We are invited to 'cast our burdens on the Lord',
with the promise, 'he will sustain you.'
The emphasis is on 'sustain' – that means to
strengthen and nourish you throughout.

Psalm 55:22
1 Peter 5:7

KEEP GOING

If you're going through hell – don't stop,
keep going!

Isaiah 43:2
Matthew 24:13

WAIT FOR THE MORNING

The psalmist provides this wonderful verse:
'Weeping may endure for the night, but joy
comes in the morning.'

Psalm 30:5

HEAD FOR THE STARS

'Two men looked out of prison bars,
one saw mud, the other saw stars.'

Deuteronomy 4:19

Psalm 121:1

YOU HAVE AN INVISIBLE FRIEND

Unseen by us, within the spiritual realm at any
time needed, God sends his angels of hope to bring
us invincible help. You are not alone.

Psalm 91:11
Psalm 34:7

FOOTPRINTS IN THE SAND

When you think your prayers are not being
answered and you see only one set of footprints in
the sand, be assured they're not yours – God is
carrying you, and your load.

Isaiah 53:4

GOD IS OMNIPRESENT

Since Jesus Christ is 'the same yesterday, today and forever', we can take the Christ of yesterday; walk with him today, and ask him to guide our paths for tomorrow – for he's already there.

Hebrews 13:8
Psalm 139:7

GOD HAS A PLAN FOR YOU

'For I know the thoughts I think towards you,'
says the Lord, 'thoughts of peace and not of evil,
to give you a future and a hope.'

Jeremiah 29:11

LEAN ON GOD

To put your faith in God is to lean your whole weight upon him. It also means removing the crutch.

Proverbs 3:4,5

GOOD THINGS COME TO THOSE
WHO WAIT

'Those who wait on the Lord shall renew their
strength; they shall mount up with wings like
eagles. They shall run and not be weary,
they shall walk and not faint.'

Isaiah 40:37

LET GOD WORK IT OUT

Leaving the details of your future in God's hands
is the most responsible act of obedience you can
make. It's also the ultimate act of faith.

Romans 8:28

BE SPIRIT LED

'Trust in the Lord with all your heart and lean not on your own understanding; in all your ways acknowledge him and he shall direct your paths.'

Proverbs 3:5–6

AVOID A QUICK FIX

When we present our problems to God
he doesn't give temporary relief,
he offers a permanent solution.

2 Thessalonians 2:16
Isaiah 26:4
Isaiah 60:19,20

SAVED BY GRACE

'Amazing Grace, how sweet the sound
that saved a wretch like me,
I once was lost but now am found
Was blind but now I see.'

Isaac Watts

Ephesians 2:5,8

HOPE CHANGES THE WORLD

'Everything that is done in the world
is done by hope.'

Martin Luther King

Ecclesiastes 9:4
Romans 8:24

CHERISH YOUR EXPERIENCES

Experience comes by persevering through life's
encounters. It is a valuable asset. Every addition
to it enhances your life.

James 1:2

LOOK TO THE LIGHT

No one ever damaged their eyesight
by looking on the brighter side of life.

2 Corinthians 4:18
Isaiah 45:22

SUBMIT TO GOD

When we fully surrender to Christ, we begin to
look at life through his eyes, and we learn to face
the future through his strength.

James 4:7

BE A COMFORTER

When God comforts us it's not necessarily
to make us comfortable, but, once comforted, to
then go on and be a comforter to others.

2 Corinthians 1:3–5

LET GOD MOULD YOU

As the potter is to the clay, so God is to our lives.
However you might presently feel, remember,
God has not finished with you yet.

Jeremiah 18:6

EXPERIENCE A NEW LIFE

Conversion is a wonderful spiritual term.
It means rebirth – a new life. It is the ultimate
source of hope for the person who wants
a change in their life.

Luke 22:32
John 3:6